The Vegan Air Fryer Cookbook

Easy and Quick Plant-Based Meals for Healthier Homemade Cooking

Devin Whiteley

CONTENTS

Louisiana-Style Eggplant Cutlets

(Ready in about 45 minutes | Servings 3)

Nutrition Facts: 214 Calories; 1.3g Fat; 43g Carbs; 6.1g Protein; 16.8g

Sugars

Ingredients

- 1 pound eggplant, cut lengthwise into 1/2-inch thick slices
- 1/4 cup plain flour
- 1/4 cup almond milk
- 1 cup fresh bread crumbs
- 1 teaspoon Cajun seasoning mix
- Sea salt and ground black pepper, to taste
- 1 cup tomato sauce
- 1 teaspoon brown mustard
- 1/2 teaspoon chili powder

Instructions

Toss your eggplant with 1 teaspoon of salt and leave it for 30 minutes; drain and rinse the eggplant and set it aside.

In a shallow bowl, mix the flour with almond milk until well combined. In a separate bowl, mix the breadcrumbs with Cajun seasoning mix, salt and black pepper.

Dip your eggplant in the flour mixture, then, coat each slice with the breadcrumb mixture, pressing to adhere.

Cook the breaded eggplant at 400 degrees F for 10 minutes, flipping them halfway through the cooking time to ensure even browning.

In the meantime, mix the remaining ingredients for the sauce. Divide the tomato mixture between eggplant cutlets and continue to cook for another 5 minutes or until thoroughly cooked.

Transfer the warm eggplant cutlets to a wire rack to stay crispy. Bon appétit!

Fried Green Beans

(Ready in about 10 minutes | Servings 2)

Nutrition Facts: 162 Calories; 11.3g Fat; 13g Carbs; 4.1g Protein; 6g Sugars

Ingredients

- 1/2 pound green beans, cleaned and trimmed
- 1 teaspoon extra-virgin olive oil
- 1/2 teaspoon onion powder
- 1/2 teaspoon shallot powder
- 1/4 teaspoon cumin powder
- 1/2 teaspoon cayenne pepper
- 1/2 teaspoon garlic powder
- Himalayan salt and freshly ground black pepper, to taste
- 1 tablespoon lime juice
- 1 tablespoon soy sauce
- 1/4 cup pecans, roughly chopped

Instructions

Toss the green beans with olive oil, spices and lime juice.

Cook the green beans in your Air Fryer at 400 degrees F for 5 minutes, shaking the basket halfway through the cooking time to promote even cooking.

Toss the green beans with soy sauce and serve garnished with chopped pecans. Bon appétit!

Famous Everything Bagel Kale Chips

(Ready in about 12 minutes | Servings 1)

Nutrition Facts: 134 Calories; 7.3g Fat; 12.1g Carbs; 7.5g Protein; 3.4g

Sugars

Ingredients

- 2 cups loosely packed kale leaves, stems removed
- 1 teaspoon olive oil
- 1 tablespoon nutritional yeast flakes
- Coarse salt and ground black pepper, to taste
- 1 teaspoon sesame seeds, lightly toasted
- 1/2 teaspoon poppy seeds, lightly toasted
- 1/4 teaspoon garlic powder

Instructions

Toss the kale leaves with olive oil, nutritional yeast, salt and black pepper.

Cook your kale at 250 degrees F for 12 minutes, shaking the basket every 4 minutes to promote even cooking.

Place the kale leaves on a platter and sprinkle evenly with sesame seeds, poppy seeds and garlic powder while still hot. Enjoy!

Portobello Mushroom Schnitzel

(Ready in about 10 minutes | Servings 2)

Nutrition Facts: 156 Calories; 1.4g Fat; 27.1g Carbs; 7.2g Protein; 5g

Sugars

Ingredients

- 7 ounces Portobello mushrooms
- 1/4 cup chickpea flour
- 1/4 cup plain flour
- 1/3 cup beer
- 1 cup breadcrumbs
- 1/2 teaspoon porcini powder
- 1/2 teaspoon dried basil
- 1/4 teaspoon dried oregano
- 1/4 teaspoon ground cumin
- 1/4 teaspoon ground bay leaf
- 1/2 teaspoon garlic powder
- 1/2 teaspoon shallot powder
- Kosher salt and ground black pepper, to taste

Instructions

Pat dry the Portobello mushrooms and set them aside.

Then, add the flour and beer to a rimmed plate and mix to combine well. In another bowl, mix the breadcrumbs with spices.

Dip your mushrooms in the flour mixture, then, coat them with the breadcrumb mixture.

Cook the breaded mushrooms in the preheated Air Fryer at 380 degrees F for 6 to 7 minutes, flipping them over halfway through the cooking time. Eat warm.

Pearl Onions with Tahini Sauce

(Ready in about 10 minutes | Servings 2)

Nutrition Facts: 226 Calories; 3.3g Fat; 23.5g Carbs; 5.5g Protein; 14.1g

Sugars

Ingredients

- 3/4 pound pearl onions
- 1 teaspoon olive oil
- Sea salt and ground black pepper, to taste
- 1/2 teaspoon thyme
- 2 tablespoons tahini
- 2 tablespoons soy sauce
- 1 tablespoon balsamic vinegar

Instructions

Toss the pearl onions with olive oil, salt, black pepper and thyme.

Cook the pearl onions in the preheated Air Fryer at 400 degrees F for 5 minutes. Shake the basket and continue to cook for another 5 minutes.

Meanwhile, make the tahini sauce by whisking the remaining ingredients;

whisk to combine well. Spoon the tahini sauce over the pearl onions and enjoy!

Fried Parsnip with Mint Yogurt Sauce

(Ready in about 10 minutes | Servings 2)

Nutrition Facts: 141 Calories; 2.8g Fat; 24.6g Carbs; 6.2g Protein; 8.2g

Sugars

Ingredients

- 1/2 parsnip, peeled and sliced into sticks
- 1 teaspoon olive oil
- Sea salt and ground black pepper, to taste
- 3 ounces Greek-style dairy-free yogurt, unsweetened
- 1 teaspoon juice
- 1/2 teaspoon fresh garlic, pressed
- 1 teaspoon fresh mint, chopped

Instructions

Toss your parsnip with olive oil, salt and black pepper.

Cook the parsnip in the preheated Air Fryer at 390 degrees F for 15 minutes, shaking the basket halfway through the cooking time.

In the meantime, mix the remaining ingredients until well combined. Serve the warm parsnip with the mint yogurt for dipping. Bon appétit!

Authentic Vegan Ratatouille

(Ready in about 15 minutes | Servings 2)

Nutrition Facts: 136 Calories; 7.4g Fat; 16g Carbs; 3.7g Protein; 8.3g

Sugars

Ingredients

- 4 ounces courgette, sliced
- 4 ounces eggplant, sliced
- 1 bell pepper, sliced
- 4 ounces tomatoes, peeled and quartered
- 1 yellow onion, peeled and sliced
- 1 teaspoon fresh garlic, minced
- 1/2 teaspoon oregano
- 1/2 teaspoon basil
- Coarse sea salt and ground black pepper, to taste
- 1 tablespoon olive oil

Instructions

Place the sliced veggies in the Air Fryer cooking basket. Season your veggies with oregano, basil, salt and black pepper. Drizzle olive oil over the top.

Cook your veggies at 400 degrees F for about 15 minutes, shaking the basket halfway through the cooking time to promote even cooking.

Arrange the sliced veggies in alternating patterns and serve warm. Bon appétit!

Peppers Provençal with Garbanzo Beans

(Ready in about 25 minutes | Servings 3)

Nutrition Facts: 236 Calories; 5.9g Fat; 40.1g Carbs; 10.1g Protein; 15.1g

Sugars

Ingredients

- 1 pound bell peppers, deseeded and sliced
- 2 teaspoons olive oil
- 1 teaspoon Herbs de Provence
- 1 onion, chopped
- 10 ounces canned tomato sauce
- 1 teaspoon red wine vinegar
- 9 ounces canned garbanzo beans

Instructions

Drizzle the bell peppers with 1 teaspoon of olive oil; sprinkle them with Herbs de Provence and transfer to the Air Fryer cooking basket.

Cook the peppers in the preheated Air Fryer at 400 degrees F for 15 minutes, shaking the basket halfway through the cooking time.

Meanwhile, heat the remaining teaspoon of olive oil in a saucepan over medium-high heat. Once hot, sauté the onion until just tender and translucent.

Then, add in the tomato sauce and let it simmer, partially covered, for about 10 minutes until the sauce has thickened. Remove from the heat and add in the vinegar and garbanzo beans; stir to combine.

Serve the roasted peppers with the saucy garbanzo beans. Bon appétit!

Crispy Garlic Tofu with Brussels Sprouts

(Ready in about 20 minutes | Servings 2)

Nutrition Facts: 256 Calories; 12.5g Fat; 21.1g Carbs; 22.8g Protein; 3.6g

Sugars

Ingredients

- 8 ounces firm tofu, pressed and cut into bite-sized cubes
- 1 teaspoon garlic paste
- 1 tablespoons arrowroot powder
- 1 teaspoon peanut oil
- 1/2 pound Brussels sprouts, halved
- Sea salt and ground black pepper, to taste

Instructions

Toss the tofu cubes with the garlic paste, arrowroot powder and peanut oil.

Transfer your tofu to the Air Fryer cooking basket; add in the Brussels sprouts and season everything with salt and black pepper.

Cook the tofu cubes and Brussels sprouts at 380 degrees F for 15 minutes, shaking the basket halfway through the cooking time. Bon appétit!

Baby Potatoes with Garlic-Rosemary Sauce

(Ready in about 50 minutes | Servings 3)

Nutrition Facts: 166 Calories; 4.6g Fat; 28.1g Carbs; 3.5g Protein; 1.6g

Sugars

Ingredients

- 1 pound baby potatoes, scrubbed
- 1 tablespoon olive oil
- 1/2 garlic bulb, slice the top 1/4-inch off the garlic head
- 1 tablespoon fresh rosemary leaves, chopped
- 1 teaspoon sherry vinegar
- 1/2 cup white wine
- Salt and freshly ground black pepper

Instructions

Brush the baby potatoes with olive oil and transfer them to the air Fryer cooking basket. Cook the baby potatoes at 400 degrees F for 12 minutes,

shaking the basket halfway through the cooking time.

Place the garlic bulb into the center of a piece of aluminum foil. Drizzle the garlic bulb with a nonstick cooking spray and wrap tightly in foil.

Cook the garlic at 390 degrees F for about 25 minutes or until the cloves are tender.

Let it cool for about 10 minutes; remove the cloves by squeezing them out of the skins; mash the garlic and add it to a saucepan.

Stir the remaining ingredients into the saucepan and let it simmer for 10 to 15 minutes until the sauce has reduced by half. Spoon the sauce over the baby potatoes and serve warm. Bon appétit!

Quinoa-Stuffed Winter Squash

(Ready in about 30 minutes | Servings 2)

Nutrition Facts: 279 Calories; 5.1g Fat; 53.1g Carbs; 8.7g Protein; 1.3g

Sugars

Ingredients

- 1/2 cup quinoa
- 1 cup loosely mixed greens, torn into small pieces
- 1 teaspoon sesame oil
- 1 clove garlic, pressed
- 1 small winter squash, halved lengthwise, seeds removed
- Sea salt and ground black pepper, to taste
- 1 tablespoon fresh parsley, roughly chopped

Instructions

Rinse your quinoa, drain it and transfer to a pot with 1 cup of lightly salted water; bring to a boil.

Turn the heat to a simmer and continue to cook, covered, for about 10 minutes; add in the mixed greens and continue to cook for 5 minutes longer.

Stir in the sesame oil and garlic and stir to combine. Divide the quinoa mixture between the winter squash halves and sprinkle it with the salt and pepper.

Cook your squash in the preheated Air Fryer at 400 degrees F for about 12 minutes.

Place the stuffed squash on individual plates, garnish with fresh parsley and serve. Bon appétit!

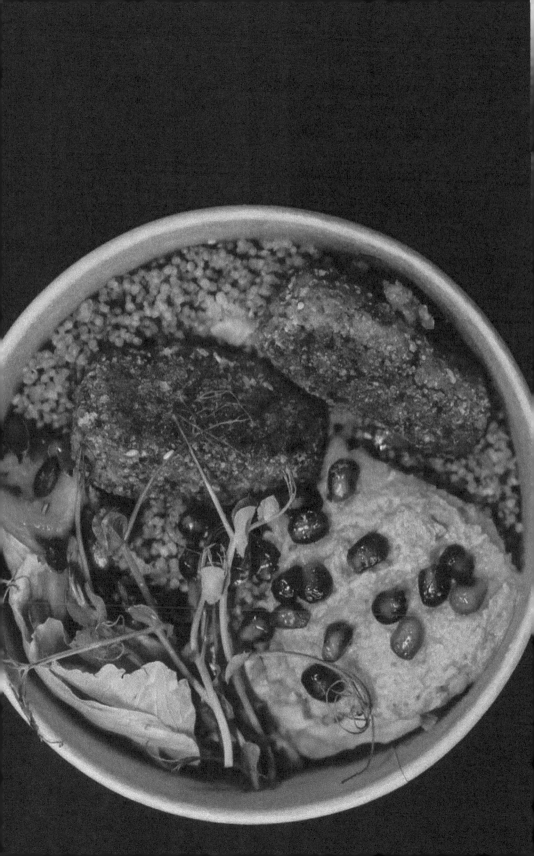

Italian-Style Tomato Cutlets

(Ready in about 10 minutes | Servings 2)

Nutrition Facts: 181 Calories; 2.6g Fat; 32.2g Carbs; 6.1g Protein; 4.1g

Sugars

Ingredients

- 1 beefsteak tomato – sliced into halves
- 1/2 cup all-purpose flour
- 1/2 cup almond milk
- 1/2 cup breadcrumbs
- 1 teaspoon Italian seasoning mix

Instructions

Pat the beefsteak tomato dry and set it aside.

In a shallow bowl, mix the all-purpose flour with almond milk. In another bowl, mix breadcrumbs with Italian seasoning mix.

Dip the beefsteak tomatoes in the flour mixture; then, coat the beefsteak tomatoes with the breadcrumb mixture, pressing to adhere to both sides.

Cook your tomatoes at 360 degrees F for about 5 minutes; turn them over and cook on the other side for 5 minutes longer. Serve at room temperature and enjoy!

Paprika Squash Fries

(Ready in about 15 minutes | Servings 3)

Nutrition Facts: 202 Calories; 5.8g Fat; 30.2g Carbs; 8.1g Protein; 2.9g

Sugars

Ingredients

- 1/4 cup rice milk
- 1/4 cup almond flour
- 2 tablespoons nutritional yeast
- 1/4 teaspoon shallot powder
- 1/2 teaspoon garlic powder
- 1/2 teaspoon paprika
- Sea salt and ground black pepper, to taste
- 1 pound butternut squash, peeled and into sticks
- 1 cup tortilla chips, crushed

Instructions

In a bowl, thoroughly combine the milk flour, nutritional yeast and spices. In another shallow bowl, place the crushed tortilla chips.

Dip the butternut squash sticks into the batter and then, roll them over the crushed tortilla chips until well coated.

Arrange the squash pieces in the Air Fryer cooking basket. Cook the squash fries at 400 degrees F for about 12 minutes, shaking the basket once or twice. Bon appétit!

Authentic Platanos Maduros

(Ready in about 15 minutes | Servings 2)

Nutrition Facts: 129 Calories; 2.5g Fat; 28.2g Carbs; 1.1g Protein; 13.4g

Sugars

Ingredients

- 1 very ripe, sweet plantain
- 1 teaspoon Caribbean Sorrel Rum Spice Mix
- 1 teaspoon coconut oil, melted

Instructions

Cut your plantain into slices.

Toss your plantain with Caribbean Sorrel Rum Spice Mix and coconut oil.

Cook your plantain in the preheated Air Fryer at 400 degrees F for 10 minutes, shaking the cooking basket halfway through the cooking time.

Serve immediately and enjoy!

Southwestern Fried Apples

(Ready in about 10 minutes | Servings 3)

Nutrition Facts: 140 Calories; 4.7g Fat; 24.2g Carbs; 0.5g Protein; 18.4g

Sugars

Ingredients

- 2 granny smith apples, peeled, cored and sliced
- 1 tablespoon coconut oil
- 1 teaspoon fresh lemon juice
- 1/4 cup brown sugar
- 1 teaspoon apple pie seasoning mix

Instructions

Toss the apple slices with the coconut oil, lemon juice, brown sugar and apple pie seasoning mix.

Place the apple slices in the Air Fryer cooking basket and cook them at 360

degrees F for about 8 minutes, shaking the cooking basket halfway through the cooking time.

Bon appétit!

Buffalo Cauliflower Bites

(Ready in about 35 minutes | Servings 2)

Nutrition Facts: 195 Calories; 2.7g Fat; 36g Carbs; 8.1g Protein; 6.5g

Sugars

Ingredients

- 1/2 pound cauliflower florets
- 1/2 cup all-purpose flour
- 1/2 cup rice milk
- 1/2 teaspoon chili powder
- 1 teaspoon garlic powder
- Sea salt and ground black pepper, to taste

Instructions

Pat the cauliflower florets dry and reserve.

In a mixing bowl, thoroughly combine the flour, rice milk, chili powder, garlic powder, salt and black pepper.

Dip the cauliflower florets in the batter until well coated on all sides. Place

the cauliflower florets in your freezer for 15 minutes.

Cook the cauliflower in the preheated Air Fryer at 390 degrees F for about 10 minutes; turn them over and cook for another 10 minutes.

Taste, adjust the seasonings and serve warm. Bon appétit!

Green Potato Croquettes

(Ready in about 45 minutes | Servings 2)

Nutrition Facts: 137 Calories; 2.9g Fat; 25.2g Carbs; 4.1g Protein; 2.8g

Sugars

Ingredients

- 1/2 pound cup russet potatoes
- 1 teaspoon olive oil
- 1/2 teaspoon garlic, pressed
- 2 cups loosely packed mixed greens, torn into pieces
- 2 tablespoons oat milk
- Sea salt and ground black pepper, to taste
- 1/4 teaspoon red pepper flakes, crushed

Instructions

Cook your potatoes for about 30 minutes until they are fork-tender; peel the potatoes and add them to a mixing bowl.

Mash your potatoes and stir in the remaining ingredients.

Shape the mixture into bite-sized balls and place them in the cooking basket; sprits the balls with a nonstick cooking oil.

Cook the croquettes at 390 degrees F for about 13 minutes, shaking the

cooking basket halfway through the cooking time.

Serve with tomato ketchup if desired. Bon appétit!

Old-Fashioned Potato Wedges

(Ready in about 15 minutes | Servings 2)

Nutrition Facts: 184 Calories; 2.4g Fat; 37.2g Carbs; 4.3g Protein; 1.6g

Sugars

Ingredients

- 2 medium potatoes, scrubbed and cut into wedges
- 1 teaspoon olive oil
- 1 teaspoon garlic powder
- 1 teaspoon shallot powder
- 1/4 teaspoon cayenne pepper
- Kosher salt and ground black pepper, to season

Instructions

Toss the potato wedges with olive oil and spices and transfer them to the Air Fryer cooking basket.

Cook the potato wedges at 400 degrees F for 6 minutes; shake the basket and cook for another 6 to 8 minutes.

Serve with your favorite vegan dip. Bon appétit!

Easy Homemade Falafel

(Ready in about 15 minutes | Servings 3)

Nutrition Facts: 274 Calories; 4.2g Fat; 46.7g Carbs; 14.3g Protein; 8.9g

Sugars

Ingredients

- 1 cup dry chickpeas, soaked overnight
- 1 small onion, sliced
- 2 tablespoons fresh cilantro
- 2 tablespoons fresh parsley
- 2 cloves garlic
- 1/2 teaspoon cayenne pepper
- Sea salt and ground black pepper, to taste
- 1/2 teaspoon ground cumin

Instructions

Drain and rinse your chickpeas and place them in a bowl of a food processor.

Add in the remaining ingredients and blitz until the **Ingredients** form a coarse meal. Roll the mixture into small balls with oiled hands.

Cook your falafel in the preheated Air Fryer at 395 degrees F for 5 minutes; turn them over and cook for another 5 to 6 minutes. Bon appétit!

Italian-Style Pasta Chips

(Ready in about 15 minutes | Servings 2)

Nutrition Facts: 224 Calories; 3.4g Fat; 43.4g Carbs; 6.1g Protein; 0.1g

Sugars

Ingredients

- 1 cup dry rice pasta
- 1 teaspoon olive oil
- 1 tablespoon nutritional yeast
- 1/2 teaspoon dried oregano
- 1/2 teaspoon dried basil
- 1 teaspoon dried parsley flakes
- Kosher salt and ground black pepper, to taste

Instructions

Cook the pasta according to the manufacturer's instructions. Drain your pasta and toss it with the remaining ingredients.

Cook the pasta chips at 390 degrees F for about 10 minutes, shaking the cooking basket halfway through the cooking time.

The pasta chips will crisp up as it cools.

Serve with tomato ketchup if desired. Bon appétit!

Shawarma Roasted Chickpeas

(Ready in about 20 minutes | Servings 2)

Nutrition Facts: 217 Calories; 9.4g Fat; 25.4g Carbs; 8g Protein; 4.5g

Sugars

Ingredients

- 8 ounces canned chickpeas
- 1/4 teaspoon turmeric powder
- 1/4 teaspoon cinnamon
- 1/4 teaspoon allspice
- 1/2 teaspoon ground coriander
- 1/4 teaspoon ground ginger
- 1/4 teaspoon smoked paprika
- Coarse sea salt and freshly ground black pepper, to taste

Instructions

Rinse your chickpeas with cold running water and pat it dry using kitchen towels.

Place the spices in a plastic bag; add in the chickpeas and shake until all the chickpeas are coated with the spices.

Spritz the spiced chickpeas with a nonstick cooking oil and transfer them to the Air Fryer cooking basket.

Cook your chickpeas in the preheated Air Fryer at 395 degrees F for 13 minutes. Turn your Air Fryer to 350 degrees F and cook an additional 6 minutes.

Bon appétit!

Spicy Sesame Cauliflower Steaks

(Ready in about 25 minutes | Servings 2)

Nutrition Facts: 247 Calories; 0.8g Fat; 54.4g Carbs; 6.6g Protein; 10.1g

Sugars

Ingredients

- 1/2 pound cauliflower, cut into 2 slabs
- 1/2 cup plain flour
- 1/4 cup cornstarch
- 1/2 cup ale
- 1/2 teaspoon hot sauce
- 1/4 teaspoon onion powder
- 1/2 teaspoon garlic powder
- 1/2 teaspoon smoked paprika
- 1 tablespoon sesame seeds
- Kosher salt and ground black pepper, to taste
- 1/4 cup buffalo sauce

Instructions

Parboil the cauliflower in the pot with a lightly salted water for about 15 minutes.

In a mixing bowl, combine the remaining ingredients, except for the buffalo sauce, until everything is well incorporated. Then, dip the cauliflower steaks into the batter.

Cook the cauliflower steaks at 400 degrees F for 10 minutes, flipping them over halfway through the cooking time to promote even cooking.

Serve the warm cauliflower steaks with buffalo sauce and enjoy!

Perfect Shallot Rings

(Ready in about 15 minutes | Servings 2)

Nutrition Facts: 347 Calories; 4.3g Fat; 66.1g Carbs; 11g Protein; 8.8g

Sugars

Ingredients

- 1/2 cup all-purpose flour
- 1/4 cup cornflour
- 1/2 cup rice milk
- 1/4 cup fizzy water
- 1/4 teaspoon turmeric powder
- Sea salt and red pepper, to taste
- 1/2 cup seasoned breadcrumbs
- 2 shallots, sliced into rings

Instructions

In a shallow bowl, thoroughly combine the flour, milk, fizzy water, turmeric, salt and pepper. In another bowl, place seasoned breadcrumbs.

Dip the shallot rings in the flour mixture; then, coat the rings with the seasoned breadcrumbs, pressing to adhere.

Transfer the shallot rings to the Air Fryer cooking basket and spritz them with a nonstick spray.

Cook the shallot rings at 380 degrees F for about 10 minutes, shaking the basket halfway through the cooking time to ensure even browning. Bon appétit!

Spicy Bean Burgers

(Ready in about 15 minutes | Servings 3)

Nutrition Facts: 227 Calories; 2.3g Fat; 40.1g Carbs; 12.1g

Protein; 2.2g

Sugars

Ingredients

- 1/2 cup old-fashioned oats
- 2 tablespoons red onions, finely chopped
- 2 garlic cloves, finely chopped
- 8 ounces canned beans
- 1/3 cup marinara sauce
- 1 teaspoon tamari sauce
- A few drops of liquid smoke
- Kosher salt and ground black pepper, to taste
- 1/4 teaspoon ancho chile powder

Instructions

Pulse all **Ingredients** in your food processor leaving some larger chunks of beans.

Now, form the mixture into patties and place them in the Air Fryer cooking basket. Brush the patties with a nonstick cooking oil.

Cook your burgers at 380 degrees F for about 15 minutes, flipping them halfway through the cooking time.

Serve on burger buns garnished with your favorite fixings. Bon appétit!

The Best Potato Fritters Ever

(Ready in about 55 minutes | Servings 3)

Nutrition Facts: 304 Calories; 6.5g Fat; 55.1g Carbs; 7.4g Protein; 2.6g

Sugars

Ingredients

- 3 medium-sized potatoes, peeled
- 1 tablespoon flax seeds, ground
- 1/2 cup plain flour
- 1/2 teaspoon cayenne pepper
- 1/4 teaspoon dried dill weed
- Sea salt and ground black pepper, to taste
- 1 tablespoon olive oil
- 1 tablespoon fresh chives, chopped

Instructions

Place your potatoes in the Air Fryer cooking basket and cook them at 400 degrees F for about 40 minutes, shaking the basket occasionally to

promote even cooking. Mash your potatoes with a fork or potato masher.

Make a vegan egg by mixing 1 tablespoon of ground flax seeds with 1 ½ tablespoons of water. Let it stand for 5 minutes.

Stir in the mashed potatoes, flour and spices; form the mixture into equal patties and brush them with olive oil.

Cook your fritters at 390 degrees F for about 10 minutes, flipping them halfway through the cooking time.

Garnish with fresh, chopped chives and serve warm. Bon appétit!

Bell Pepper Fries

(Ready in about 15 minutes | Servings 2)

Nutrition Facts: 392 Calories; 5.5g Fat; 71.1g Carbs; 13.4g Protein; 11.1g

Sugars

Ingredients

- 1 cup flour
- 1 cup oat milk
- 1/2 teaspoon dried marjoram
- 1/2 teaspoon turmeric powder
- Sea salt and ground black pepper, to taste
- 1 cup seasoned breadcrumbs
- 2 large bell peppers

Instructions

In a shallow bowl, thoroughly combine the flour, milk, marjoram, turmeric, salt and black pepper. In another bowl, place seasoned breadcrumbs.

Dip the pepper rings in the flour mixture; then, coat the rings with the seasoned breadcrumbs, pressing to adhere.

Transfer the pepper rings to the Air Fryer cooking basket and spritz them with a nonstick spray.

Cook the pepper rings at 380 degrees F for about 10 minutes, shaking the basket halfway through the cooking time to promote even cooking. Bon appétit!

Polish Placki Ziemniaczan

(Ready in about 10 minutes | Servings 2)

Nutrition Facts: 262 Calories; 3.7g Fat; 50.1g Carbs; 6.4g Protein; 10.3g

Sugars

Ingredients

- 1/2 pound potatoes, peeled and finely grated
- 1/2 small white onion, finely chopped
- 1/4 cup all-purpose flour
- 1/2 teaspoon turmeric powder
- 2 tablespoons breadcrumbs
- Kosher salt and freshly ground black pepper, to taste
- 2 tablespoons granulated sugar
- 2 ounces sour cream

Instructions

Place the grated potatoes in a triple layer of cheesecloth; now, twist and squeeze the potatoes until no more liquid comes out of them.

Place the potatoes in a mixing bowl; stir in the onion, flour, turmeric powder, breadcrumbs, salt and black pepper.

Cook them at 380 degrees for about 10 minutes, turning over after 5 minutes. Serve with granulated sugar and sour cream. Enjoy!

Favorite Lentil Burgers

(Ready in about 15 minutes | Servings 3)

Nutrition Facts: 195 Calories; 4.8g Fat; 31.1g Carbs; 8.9g Protein; 9.8g

Sugars

Ingredients

- 1/2 cup wild rice, cooked
- 1 cup red lentils, cooked
- 1/2 small onion, quartered
- 1/2 small beet, peeled and quartered
- 1 garlic clove
- 1/4 cup walnuts
- 2 tablespoons breadcrumbs
- 1/2 teaspoon cayenne pepper
- Sea salt and ground black pepper, to taste
- 1 tablespoon vegan barbecue sauce

Instructions

In your food processor, pulse all **Ingredients** until a moldable dough forms.

Shape the mixture into equal patties and place them in the lightly oiled Air Fryer cooking basket.

Cook your burgers at 380 degrees F for about 15 minutes, flipping them halfway through the cooking time.

Serve on burger buns and enjoy!

Traditional Indian Pakora

(Ready in about 35 minutes | Servings 2)

Nutrition Facts: 175 Calories; 4.4g Fat; 24.6g Carbs; 9.5g Protein; 3.9g

Sugars

Ingredients

- 1 large zucchini, grated
- 1/2 cup besan flour
- 1/2 teaspoon baking powder
- 2 scallion stalks, chopped
- 1/2 teaspoon paprika
- 1/4 teaspoon curry powder
- 14 teaspoon ginger-garlic paste
- Sea salt and ground black pepper, to taste
- 1 teaspoon olive oil

Instructions

Sprinkle the salt over the grated zucchini and leave it for 20 minutes. Then, squeeze the zucchini and drain off the excess liquid.

Mix the grated zucchini with the flour, baking powder, scallions, paprika, curry powder and ginger-garlic paste. Salt and pepper to taste.

Shape the mixture into patties and transfer them to the Air Fryer cooking basket. Brush the zucchini patties with 1 teaspoon of olive oil.

Cook the pakora at 380 degrees F for about 12 minutes, flipping them halfway through the cooking time.

Serve on dinner rolls and enjoy!

The Best Crispy Tofu

(Ready in about 55 minutes | Servings 4)

Nutrition Facts: 245 Calories; 13.3g Fat; 16.7g Carbs; 18.2g Protein; 1.2g

Sugars

Ingredients

- 16 ounces firm tofu, pressed and cubed
- 1 tablespoon vegan oyster sauce
- 1 tablespoon tamari sauce
- 1 teaspoon cider vinegar
- 1 teaspoon pure maple syrup
- 1 teaspoon sriracha
- 1/2 teaspoon shallot powder
- 1/2 teaspoon porcini powder
- 1 teaspoon garlic powder
- 1 tablespoon sesame oil
- 5 tablespoons cornstarch

Instructions

Toss the tofu with the oyster sauce, tamari sauce, vinegar, maple syrup, sriracha, shallot powder, porcini powder, garlic powder, and sesame oil. Let it marinate for 30 minutes.

Toss the marinated tofu with the cornstarch.

Cook at 360 degrees F for 10 minutes; turn them over and cook for 12 minutes more. Bon appétit!

Rainbow Roasted Vegetables

(Ready in about 25 minutes | Servings 4)

Nutrition Facts: 333 Calories; 23.4g Fat; 25.9g Carbs; 8.7g Protein; 8g

Sugars

Ingredients

- 1 red bell pepper, seeded and cut into 1/2-inch chunks
- 1 cup squash, peeled and cut into 1/2-inch chunks
- 1 yellow bell pepper, seeded and cut into 1/2-inch chunks
- 1 yellow onion, quartered
- 1 green bell pepper, seeded and cut into 1/2-inch chunks
- 1 cup broccoli, broken into 1/2-inch florets
- 2 parsnips, trimmed and cut into 1/2-inch chunks
- 2 garlic cloves, minced
- Pink Himalayan salt and ground black pepper, to taste
- 1/2 teaspoon marjoram
- 1/2 teaspoon dried oregano
- 1/4 cup dry white wine
- 1/4 cup vegetable broth

- 1/2 cup Kalamata olives, pitted and sliced

Instructions

Arrange your vegetables in a single layer in the baking pan in the order of the rainbow (red, orange, yellow, and green). Scatter the minced garlic around the vegetables.

Season with salt, black pepper, marjoram, and oregano. Drizzle the white wine and vegetable broth over the vegetables.

Roast in the preheated Air Fryer at 390 degrees F for 15 minutes, rotating the pan once or twice.

Scatter the Kalamata olives all over your vegetables and serve warm. Bon appétit!

rispy Butternut Squash Fries

(Ready in about 25 minutes | Servings 4)

Nutrition Facts: 288 Calories; 7.6g Fat; 45.6g Carbs; 11.4g Protein; 3.1g

Sugars

Ingredients

- 1 cup all-purpose flour
- Salt and ground black pepper, to taste
- 3 tablespoons nutritional yeast flakes
- 1/2 cup almond milk
- 1/2 cup almond meal
- 1/2 cup bread crumbs
- 1 tablespoon herbs (oregano, basil, rosemary), chopped
- 1 pound butternut squash, peeled and cut into French fry shapes

Instructions

In a shallow bowl, combine the flour, salt, and black pepper. In another shallow dish, mix the nutritional yeast flakes with the almond milk until well combined.

Mix the almond meal, breadcrumbs, and herbs in a third shallow dish.

Dredge the butternut squash in the flour mixture, shaking off the excess.

Then, dip in the milk mixture; lastly, dredge in the breadcrumb mixture.

Spritz the butternut squash fries with cooking oil on all sides.

Cook in the preheated Air Fryer at 400 degrees F approximately 12 minutes, turning them over halfway through the cooking time.

Serve with your favorite sauce for dipping. Bon appétit!

Easy Crispy Shawarma Chickpeas

(Ready in about 25 minutes | Servings 4)

Nutrition Facts: 150 Calories; 8.7g Fat; 14.2g Carbs; 4.4g Protein; 2.5g

Sugars

Ingredients

- 1 (12-ounce) can chickpeas, drained and rinsed
- 2 tablespoons canola oil
- 1 teaspoon cayenne pepper
- 1 teaspoon sea salt
- 1 tablespoon Shawarma spice blend

Instructions

Toss all **Ingredients** in a mixing bowl.

Roast in the preheated Air Fryer at 380 degrees F for 10 minutes, shaking

the basket halfway through the cooking time.

Work in batches. Bon appétit!

710. Caribbean-Style Fried Plantains

(Ready in about 20 minutes | Servings 2)

Nutrition Facts: 302 Calories; 14.2g Fat; 47.9g Carbs; 1.2g Protein; 21.6g

Sugars

Ingredients

2 plantains, peeled and cut into slices

2 tablespoons avocado oil

2 teaspoons Caribbean Sorrel Rum Spice Mix

Instructions

Toss the plantains with the avocado oil and spice mix.

Cook in the preheated Air Fryer at 400 degrees F for 10 minutes, shaking the cooking basket halfway through the cooking time.

Adjust the seasonings to taste and enjoy!

Famous Buffalo Cauliflower

(Ready in about 30 minutes | Servings 4)

Nutrition Facts: 306 Calories; 8.6g Fat; 50.3g Carbs; 9.7g Protein; 12.1g

Sugars

Ingredients

- 1 pound cauliflower florets
- 1/2 cup all-purpose flour
- 1/2 cup rice flour
- Sea salt and cracked black pepper, to taste
- 1/2 teaspoon cayenne pepper
- 1/2 teaspoon chili powder
- 1/2 cup soy milk
- 2 tablespoons soy sauce
- 2 tablespoons tahini
- 1 teaspoon vegetable oil
- 2 cloves garlic, minced
- 6 scotch bonnet peppers, seeded and sliced
- 1 small-sized onion, minced
- 1/2 teaspoon salt

- 1 cup water
- 2 tablespoons white vinegar
- 1 tablespoon granulated sugar

Instructions

Rinse the cauliflower florets and pat them dry. Spritz the Air Fryer basket with cooking spray.

In a mixing bowl, combine the all purpose flour and rice flour; add the salt, black pepper, cayenne pepper, and chili powder.

Add the soy milk, soy sauce, and tahini. Stir until a thick batter is formed.

Dip the cauliflower florets in the batter.

Cook the cauliflower at 400 degrees F for 16 minutes, turning them over halfway through the cooking time.

Meanwhile, heat the vegetable oil in a saucepan over medium-high heat; then, sauté the garlic, peppers, and onion for a minute or so or until they are fragrant.

Add the remaining ingredients and bring the mixture to a rapid boil. Now, reduce the heat to simmer, and continue cooking for 10 minutes more or until the sauce has reduced by half.

Pour the sauce over the prepared cauliflower and serve. Bon appétit!

Crunchy Eggplant Rounds

(Ready in about 45 minutes | Servings 4)

Nutrition Facts: 327 Calories; 8.5g Fat; 51.9g Carbs; 12.5g Protein; 7.3g

Sugars

Ingredients

- 1 (1-pound) eggplant, sliced
- 1/2 cup flax meal
- 1/2 cup rice flour
- Coarse sea salt and ground black pepper, to taste
- 1 teaspoon paprika
- 1 cup water
- 1 cup cornbread crumbs, crushed
- 1/2 cup vegan parmesan

Instructions

Toss the eggplant with 1 tablespoon of salt and let it stand for 30 minutes.

Drain and rinse well.

Mix the flax meal, rice flour, salt, black pepper, and paprika in a bowl. Then, pour in the water and whisk to combine well.

In another shallow bowl, mix the cornbread crumbs and vegan parmesan.

Dip the eggplant slices in the flour mixture, then in the crumb mixture; press to coat on all sides. Transfer to the lightly greased Air Fryer basket.

Cook at 370 degrees F for 6 minutes. Turn each slice over and cook an additional 5 minutes.

Serve garnished with spicy ketchup if desired. Bon appétit!

Classic Vegan Chili

(Ready in about 40 minutes | Servings 3)

Nutrition Facts: 335 Calories; 17.6g Fat; 37.3g Carbs; 11.5g Protein; 6.1g

Sugars

Ingredients

- 1 tablespoon olive oil
- 1/2 yellow onion, chopped
- 2 garlic cloves, minced
- 2 red bell peppers, seeded and chopped
- 1 red chili pepper, seeded and minced
- Sea salt and ground black pepper, to taste
- 1 teaspoon ground cumin
- 1 teaspoon cayenne pepper
- 1 teaspoon Mexican oregano
- 1/2 teaspoon mustard seeds
- 1/2 teaspoon celery seeds
- 1 can (28-ounces) diced tomatoes with juice
- 1 cup vegetable broth
- 1 (15-ounce) can black beans, rinsed and drained

- 1 bay leaf

- 1 teaspoon cider vinegar

- 1 avocado, sliced

Instructions

Start by preheating your Air Fryer to 365 degrees F.

Heat the olive oil in a baking pan until sizzling. Then, sauté the onion, garlic, and peppers in the baking pan. Cook for 4 to 6 minutes.

Now, add the salt, black pepper, cumin, cayenne pepper, oregano, mustard seeds, celery seeds, tomatoes, and broth. Cook for 20 minutes, stirring every 4 minutes.

Stir in the canned beans, bay leaf, cider vinegar; let it cook for a further 8 minutes, stirring halfway through the cooking time.

Serve in individual bowls garnished with the avocado slices. Enjoy!

Dad's Roasted Pepper Salad

(Ready in about 25 minutes + chilling time | Servings 4)

Nutrition Facts: 296 Calories; 25.6g Fat; 15.6g Carbs; 4.6g Protein; 4.7g

Sugars

Ingredients

- 2 yellow bell peppers
- 2 red bell peppers
- 2 green bell peppers
- 1 Serrano pepper
- 4 tablespoons olive oil
- 2 tablespoons cider vinegar
- 2 garlic cloves, peeled and pressed
- 1 teaspoon cayenne pepper
- Sea salt, to taste
- 1/2 teaspoon mixed peppercorns, freshly crushed
- 1/2 cup pine nuts
- 1/4 cup loosely packed fresh Italian parsley leaves, roughly chopped

Instructions

Start by preheating your Air Fryer to 400 degrees F. Brush the Air Fryer basket lightly with cooking oil.

Then, roast the peppers for 5 minutes. Give the peppers a half turn; place them back in the cooking basket and roast for another 5 minutes.

Turn them one more time and roast until the skin is charred and soft or 5 more minutes. Peel the peppers and let them cool to room temperature.

In a small mixing dish, whisk the olive oil, vinegar, garlic, cayenne pepper, salt, and crushed peppercorns. Dress the salad and set aside.

Add the pine nuts to the cooking basket. Roast at 360 degrees F for 4 minutes; give the nuts a good toss. Put the cooking basket back again and roast for a further 3 to 4 minutes.

Scatter the toasted nuts over the peppers and garnish with parsley. Bon appétit!

Cinnamon Pear Chips

(Ready in about 25 minutes | Servings 1)

Nutrition Facts: 133 Calories; 0.2g Fat; 35g Carbs; 0.6g Protein; 25.2g

Sugars

Ingredients

- 1 medium pear, cored and thinly sliced
- 2 tablespoons cinnamon & sugar mixture

Instructions

Toss the pear slices with the cinnamon & sugar mixture. Transfer them to

the lightly greased Air Fryer basket.

Bake in the preheated Air Fryer at 380 degrees F for 8 minutes, turning them over halfway through the cooking time.

Transfer to wire rack to cool. Bon appétit!

Swiss Chard and Potato Fritters

(Ready in about 35 minutes | Servings 4)

Nutrition Facts: 492 Calories; 18.5g Fat; 66.7g Carbs; 16.9g Protein; 4.8g

Sugars

Ingredients

- 8 baby potatoes
- 2 tablespoons olive oil
- 1 garlic clove, pressed
- 1/2 cup leeks, chopped
- 1 cup Swiss chard, torn into small pieces
- Sea salt and ground black pepper, to your liking
- 1 tablespoon flax seed, soaked in 3 tablespoon water (vegan egg)
- 1 cup vegan cheese, shredded
- 1/4 cup chickpea flour

Instructions

Start by preheating your Air Fryer to 400 degrees F.

Drizzle olive oil all over the potatoes. Place the potatoes in the Air Fryer basket and cook approximately 15 minutes, shaking the basket periodically.

Lightly crush the potatoes to split; mash the potatoes with the other

Ingredients.

Form the potato mixture into patties.

Bake in the preheated Air Fryer at 380 degrees F for 14 minutes, flipping them halfway through the cooking time. Bon appétit!

Veggie Fajitas with Simple Guacamole

(Ready in about 25 minutes | Servings 4)

Nutrition Facts: 307 Calories; 14.3g Fat; 40.2g Carbs; 8.2g Protein; 7.5g

Sugars

Ingredients

- 1 tablespoon canola oil
- 1/2 cup scallions, thinly sliced
- 2 bell peppers, seeded and sliced into strips
- 1 habanero pepper, seeded and minced
- 1 garlic clove, minced
- 4 large Portobello mushrooms, thinly sliced
- 1/4 cup salsa
- 1 tablespoon yellow mustard
- Kosher salt and ground black pepper, to taste
- 1/2 teaspoon Mexican oregano
- 1 medium ripe avocado, peeled, pitted and mashed
- 1 tablespoon fresh lemon juice
- 1/2 teaspoon onion powder

- 1/2 teaspoon garlic powder
- 1 teaspoon red pepper flakes
- 4 (8-inch) flour tortillas

Instructions

Brush the sides and bottom of the cooking basket with canola oil. Add the

scallions and cook for 1 to 2 minutes or until aromatic.

Then, add the peppers, garlic, and mushrooms to the cooking basket. Cook for 2 to 3 minutes or until tender.

Stir in the salsa, mustard, salt, black pepper, and oregano. Cook in the preheated Air Fryer at 380 degrees F for 15 minutes, stirring occasionally.

In the meantime, make your guacamole by mixing mashed avocado together with the lemon juice, garlic powder, onion powder, and red pepper flakes.

Divide between the tortillas and garnish with guacamole. Roll up your tortillas and enjoy!

Authentic Churros with Hot Chocolate

(Ready in about 25 minutes | Servings 3)

Nutrition Facts: 432 Calories; 15.8g Fat; 63.9g Carbs; 8.4g Protein; 24.7g

Sugars

Ingredients

- 1/2 cup water

- 2 tablespoons granulated sugar

- 1/4 teaspoon sea salt

- 1 teaspoon lemon zest

- 1 tablespoon canola oil

- 1 cup all-purpose flour

- 2 ounces dark chocolate

- 1 cup milk

- 1 tablespoon cornstarch

- 1/3 cup sugar

- 1 teaspoon ground cinnamon

Instructions

To make the churro dough, boil the water in a pan over medium-high heat;

now, add the sugar, salt and lemon zest; cook until dissolved.

Add the canola oil and remove the pan from the heat. Gradually stir in the flour, whisking continuously until the mixture forms a ball.

Pour the mixture into a piping bag with a large star tip. Squeeze 4-inch strips of dough into the greased Air Fryer pan.

Cook at 410 degrees F for 6 minutes.

Meanwhile, prepare the hot chocolate for dipping. Melt the chocolate and 1/2 cup of milk in a pan over low heat.

Dissolve the cornstarch in the remaining 1/2 cup of milk; stir into the hot chocolate mixture. Cook on low heat approximately 5 minutes.

Mix the sugar and cinnamon; roll the churros in this mixture. Serve with the hot chocolate on the side. Enjoy!

Ooey-Gooey Dessert Quesadilla

(Ready in about 25 minutes | Servings 2)

Nutrition Facts: 476 Calories; 28.8g Fat; 45g Carbs; 9.2g Protein; 18.5g

Sugars

Ingredients

- 1/4 cup blueberries
- 1/4 cup fresh orange juice
- 1/2 tablespoon maple syrup
- 1/2 cup vegan cream cheese
- 1 teaspoon vanilla extract
- 2 (6-inch) tortillas
- 2 teaspoons coconut oil
- 1/4 cup vegan dark chocolate

Instructions

Bring the blueberries, orange juice, and maple syrup to a boil in a saucepan. Reduce the heat and let it simmer until the sauce thickens, about 10 minutes.

In a mixing dish, combine the cream cheese with the vanilla extract; spread on the tortillas. Add the blueberry filling on top. Fold in half.

Place the quesadillas in the greased Air Fryer basket. Cook at 390 degrees F for 10 minutes, until tortillas are golden brown and filling is melted. Make sure to turn them over halfway through the cooking.

Heat the coconut oil in a small pan and add the chocolate; whisk to combine well. Drizzle the chocolate sauce over the quesadilla and serve.

Enjoy!

Couscous with Sun-Dried Tomatoes

(Ready in about 30 minutes | Servings 4)

Nutrition Facts: 230 Calories; 4.3g Fat; 41.3g Carbs; 7.2g Protein; 0.3g

Sugars

Ingredients

- 1 cup couscous
- 1 cup boiled water
- 2 garlic cloves, pressed
- 1/3 cup coriander, chopped
- 1 cup shallots, chopped
- 4 ounces sun-dried tomato strips in oil
- 1 cup arugula lettuce, torn into pieces
- 2 tablespoons apple cider vinegar
- Sea salt and ground black pepper, to taste

Instructions

Put the couscous in a bowl; pour the boiling water, cover and set aside for 5 to 8 minutes; fluff with a fork.

Place the couscous in a lightly greased cake pan. Transfer the pan to the

Air Fryer basket and cook at 360 digress F about 20 minutes. Make sure to stir every 5 minutes to ensure even cooking.

Transfer the prepared couscous to a nice salad bowl. Add the remaining **Ingredients**; stir to combine and enjoy!

Thai Sweet Potato Balls

(Ready in about 50 minutes | Servings 4)

Nutrition Facts: 286 Calories; 6.1g Fat; 56.8g Carbs; 3.1g Protein; 33.7g

Sugars

Ingredients

- 1 pound sweet potatoes
- 1 cup brown sugar
- 1 tablespoon orange juice
- 2 teaspoons orange zest
- 1/2 teaspoon ground cinnamon
- 1/4 teaspoon ground cloves
- 1/2 cup almond meal
- 1 teaspoon baking powder
- 1 cup coconut flakes

Instructions

Bake the sweet potatoes at 380 degrees F for 30 to 35 minutes until tender; peel and mash them.

Add the brown sugar, orange juice, orange zest, ground cinnamon, cloves, almond meal, and baking powder; mix to combine well.

Roll the balls in the coconut flakes.

Bake in the preheated Air Fryer at 360 degrees F for 15 minutes or until thoroughly cooked and crispy.

Repeat the process until you run out of **Ingredients**. Bon appétit!

Easy Granola with Raisins and Nuts

(Ready in about 40 minutes | Servings 8)

Nutrition Facts: 222 Calories; 14g Fat; 29.9g Carbs; 5.3g Protein; 11.3g

Sugars

Ingredients

- 2 cups rolled oats
- 1/2 cup walnuts, chopped
- 1/3 cup almonds chopped
- 1/4 cup raisins
- 1/4 cup whole wheat pastry flour
- 1/2 teaspoon cinnamon
- 1/4 teaspoon nutmeg, preferably freshly grated
- 1/2 teaspoon salt
- 1/3 cup coconut oil, melted
- 1/3 cup agave nectar
- 1/2 teaspoon coconut extract
- 1/2 teaspoon vanilla extract

Instructions

Thoroughly combine all **Ingredients**. Then, spread the mixture onto the Air Fryer trays. Spritz with cooking spray.

Bake at 230 degrees F for 25 minutes; rotate the trays and bake 10 to 15 minutes more.

This granola can be stored in an airtight container for up to 2 weeks. Enjoy!

Indian Plantain Chips (Kerala Neenthram)

(Ready in about 30 minutes | Servings 2)

Nutrition Facts: 263 Calories; 9.4g Fat; 49.2g Carbs; 1.5g Protein; 21.3g

Sugars

Ingredients

- 1 pound plantain, thinly sliced
- 1 tablespoon turmeric
- 2 tablespoons coconut oil

Instructions

Fill a large enough cup with water and add the turmeric to the water.

Soak the plantain slices in the turmeric water for 15 minutes. Brush with coconut oil and transfer to the Air Fryer basket.

Cook in the preheated Air Fryer at 400 degrees F for 10 minutes, shaking the cooking basket halfway through the cooking time.

Serve at room temperature. Enjoy!

Aromatic Baked Potatoes with Chives

(Ready in about 45 minutes | Servings 2)

Nutrition Facts: 434 Calories; 14.1g Fat; 69g Carbs; 8.2g Protein; 5.1g

Sugars

Ingredients

- 4 medium baking potatoes, peeled
- 2 tablespoons olive oil
- 1/4 teaspoon red pepper flakes
- 1/4 teaspoon smoked paprika
- 1 tablespoon sea salt
- 2 garlic cloves, minced
- 2 tablespoons chives, chopped

Instructions

Toss the potatoes with the olive oil, seasoning, and garlic.

Place them in the Air Fryer basket. Cook in the preheated Air Fryer at 400 degrees F for 40 minutes or until fork tender.

Garnish with fresh chopped chives. Bon appétit!

Classic Baked Banana

(Ready in about 20 minutes | Servings 2)

Nutrition Facts: 202 Calories; 5.9g Fat; 40.2g Carbs; 1.1g Protein; 29g

Sugars

Ingredients

- 2 just-ripe bananas
- 2 teaspoons lime juice
- 2 tablespoons honey
- 1/4 teaspoon grated nutmeg
- 1/2 teaspoon ground cinnamon
- A pinch of salt

Instructions

Toss the banana with all **Ingredients** until well coated. Transfer your bananas to the parchment-lined cooking basket.

Bake in the preheated Air Fryer at 370 degrees F for 12 minutes, turning them over halfway through the cooking time. Enjoy!

Garlic-Roasted Brussels Sprouts with Mustard

(Ready in about 20 minutes | Servings 3)

Nutrition Facts: 151 Calories; 9.6g Fat; 14.5g Carbs; 5.4g Protein; 3.4g

Sugars

Ingredients

- 1 pound Brussels sprouts, halved
- 2 tablespoons olive oil
- Sea salt and freshly ground black pepper, to taste
- 2 garlic cloves, minced
- 1 tablespoon Dijon mustard

Instructions

Toss the Brussels sprouts with the olive oil, salt, black pepper, and garlic.

Roast in the preheated Air Fryer at 380 degrees F for 15 minutes, shaking the basket occasionally.

Serve with Dijon mustard and enjoy!

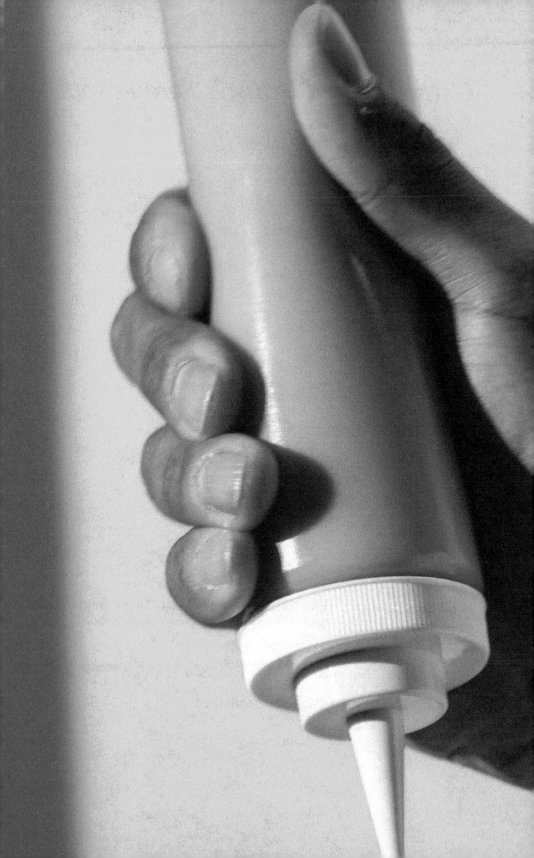

Italian-Style Risi e Bisi

(Ready in about 20 minutes | Servings 4)

Nutrition Facts: 434 Calories; 8.3g Fat; 79.8g Carbs; 9.9g Protein; 5g

Sugars

Ingredients

- 2 cups brown rice
- 4 cups water
- 1/2 cup frozen green peas
- 3 tablespoons soy sauce
- 1 tablespoon olive oil
- 1 cup brown mushrooms, sliced
- 2 garlic cloves, minced
- 1 small-sized onion, chopped
- 1 tablespoon fresh parsley, chopped

Instructions

Heat the brown rice and water in a pot over high heat. Bring it to a boil; turn the stove down to simmer and cook for 35 minutes. Allow your rice to cool completely.

Transfer the cold cooked rice to the lightly greased Air Fryer pan. Add the remaining ingredients and stir to combine.

Cook in the preheated Air Fryer at 360 degrees F for 18 to 22 minutes.

Serve warm.